Jack
and the
Giant Moa

A graphic novel

Story by Phillip Simpson
Illustrations by Jim Crawley

T0362828

Jack and the Giant Moa

Text: Phillip Simpson
Publishers: Tania Mazzeo and Eliza Webb
Series consultant: Amanda Sutera
  Hands on Heads Consulting
Editors: Laken Ballinger and Sarah Layton
Project editor: Annabel Smith
Designer: Jess Kelly
Project designer: Danielle Maccarone
Illustrations: Jim Crawley
Production controller: Renee Tome

NovaStar

Text © 2024 Cengage Learning Australia Pty Limited
Illustrations © 2024 Cengage Learning Australia Pty Limited

ISBN 978 0 17 033425 9

Cengage Learning Australia
Level 5, 80 Dorcas Street
Southbank VIC 3006 Australia
Phone: 1300 790 853
Email: aust.nelsonprimary@cengage.com

For learning solutions, visit **cengage.com.au**

Printed in China by 1010 Printing International Ltd
1 2 3 4 5 6 7 28 27 26 25 24

*Nelson acknowledges the Traditional Owners and Custodian
of the lands of all First Nations Peoples. We pay respect
to Elders past and present, and extend that respect to
all First Nations Peoples today.*

Contents

Chapter 1
Lost

It's the school holidays. Jack and Dad are about to start a hike along the Moa Park Track in Aotearoa New Zealand.

I hope we get to see some wildlife today, Dad!

Me too, Jack!

My new map app should make it easy to follow the track.

Look! A tuatara! Just like in my wildlife book.

A tuatara is a kind of reptile. They've been around since the dinosaurs!

Jack and Dad find themselves in an unfamiliar valley.

Does the bush look *different* to you?

It does. It looks ... older, somehow.

How did we get here?

I don't know. It makes no sense.

My phone still isn't working.

We should be able to find the track without the app. We didn't go that far off it.

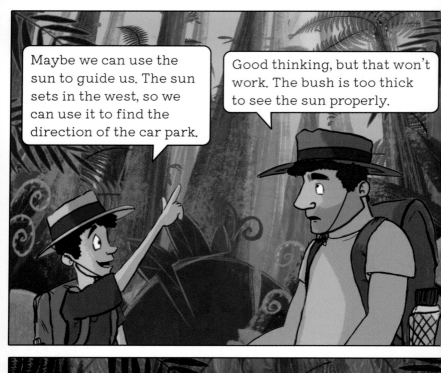

Chapter 3

Back in Time

ack and Dad can't quite believe what they're seeing ...

It looks like a giant moa. But they went extinct hundreds of years ago! I think we've ... travelled back in time.

Suddenly ...

What's that?

It's a Haast's eagle! They used to hunt the moa. We have to do something, or the eagle will eat the moa!

But what can we do?

I've got an idea! I'll do a bird call and scare away the eagle.

ack's bird call distracts e eagle and it begins fly away.

That was close. Lucky it didn't try to hunt me instead!

It's getting dark, Jack. We have to find our way out of here. And quickly! It's dangerous to spend the night here with giant eagles flying around!

But first, Jack, let me get a few pictures.

hen, something strange happens ...

The moa is coming towards us! What's it doing?

I know this sounds weird, but I think the moa wants us to follow it.

Maybe it wants to help us because we saved it.

Well, we haven't got a better plan ...

As the light fades, the moa leads Jack and Dad through the thick jungle.

Where's it taking us?

I'm not sure, Jack.

When the moa stops.

Look!

The moa has a baby! It must have been hiding it here, safe from the eagle.

Chapter 5

The Way Back

Suddenly, another mist descends over Jack and Dad.

The End

24